FEEDING FIRE

Feeding Fire

A Journey of the Heart

JOHN B. COBURN

MOREHOUSE-BARLOW CO.

Wilton, Connecticut

1238

The illustration which comprises the dust jacket of this book is a watercolor by Andrew Wyeth and is used with his kind permission.

Morehouse-Barlow Co., Inc.
78 Danbury Road
Wilton, Connecticut 06897

ISBN 0-8192-1281-4

Library of Congress Catalogue Card Number 80-81103

Printed in the United States of America

To
Christus
in whom
all loves
are
eternal

———

Robert M. Gilday
in memoriam

Duneloch
6 August 1980

Contents

Foreword by Douglas V. Steere   *page* 11

The Eye   17

Coming to Terms   18

The Thin Line   19

Feeding Fire   20

Identity   23

Presence   24

Fire   25

The Swing   26

A Reminder   28

Currents   29

Frail Stuff   30

Slash   31

Silence   32

Holding On   33

On Retreat   34

Junk   35

Longing   36

Honor   38

Friend or Enemy   39

Terror   41

Darkness   43

Good Friday   45

Holy Saturday   46

Easter Monday   47

Soaring   48

A Little While   49
"All Shall Be Well"   50
Birth   51
Union   52
Aching   53
Job   54
Flux   55
Tantalizer   56
Eternity   57

Foreword

I have known John Coburn for almost twenty years. For me he has always excelled in "the skill of skills" which is the guiding of souls. His fresh and authentic counsel that has come in his books on the practice of prayer and his collections of moving sermons and retreat addresses have spoken to our needs and have been able to throw a searing beam on the mixed lives that most of us are living and to invite us to "come in, come in, come still further in." I have known of his faithfulness as a pastor and have felt the warmth of his friendship. I have also been touched by his personal responses to public injustice and neglect. Now in this slender collection of spiritual poems John Coburn unsheaths for me a whole new and fresh dimension of his Christian witness and one that dares to bare his own spiritual journey beyond anything that has come before.

In the late sixteenth and early seventeenth centuries Britain produced a procession of religious poets of the stature of George Herbert and Thomas Traherne, and their gift to their centuries was not small. Seldom in our own time has a contemporary spiritual guide made use of the powerful instrument of a sheaf of prayers that spring so honestly and tellingly from the writer's imaginative core to encourage his companions on the way.

Using a form of verse that is reminiscent of Charles Peguy, these poems talk to God, wrestle with God, yield

11

to God. They are short, swift, full of the longing, the ecstasies, the temptations and trials, the failures, the darkness, but are always pointed toward the experience of being loved into submission. They call forth from us "the sharp dart of longing love." They also call forth gratitude that a fellow pilgrim who has not arrived but is still on journey has dared to unveil so movingly his own continuing search and his ever so delicately concealed invitation to join him.

Douglas V. Steere

*"The wood
of the Cross
is the best
for feeding
the fire
of love"* *

*Attributed to either
Father Andrew, S.D.C., or
Father S. C. Hughson, O.H.C.

FEEDING FIRE

The Eye

My eye
  on you
    alone.

God
  my attention
    to you
      alone.

As yours
  to me.

In your sight
  then
I go about
  my business
And yours.

Coming To Terms

Holy Lord
  great Lord
    pressing, pressing
      indomitable
      Lord

From whom
  escape
    impossible

Who
  embraces,
    holds fast,
      consumes

— all terrifying,
  intemperate one —
with whom I come to terms
on your terms
  alone

— So glory to you
  O holy Lord.

The Thin Line

The line
   the thin line
Over which
   crossing I go
Further toward you
   or away . . .

— Which way forward
   or back —
Once I knew
   now unsure
But I do know
   You are
     there

Whether forward
   or back
So keep me
   tilting toward
     You.

Feeding Fire

You promised us, Lord,
   never to ask us to do
      something without giving us
the power to do it. You did
   make this promise didn't you?

So, then, I now offer you
   everything about me
   — my sins that know
no end because sin itself
   permeates me.
   — my loves that inspire, exalt
and corrupt me because I make
   them "mine" rather than yours.
   — all violations of that
   love which is yours alone,
a free gift of grace in
   all love.

I accept, then, your
   acceptance of me, which I
      can do only because you
make it possible to do. I
   can't — don't want to — do it
      by myself. I'd rather hold out,
be in charge, negotiate a settlement
   with you. But you ask — order —
   me not to, and now by your
giving me the power to do what you
   want I do it. *You* do it.

So I am ready now to
  move on in you, deeper in
    you, telling of — showing
faith in — your love.

"The wood
  of the Cross
  is the best
  for feeding
    the fire
    of love."

The fire of love now fed by the wood
  of your cross consumes me.

Not that I put you out
  of my mind, Lord. I've
    tried that. It doesn't work.
You are imprinted on it. You
are indelible, non-eradicable,
    won't go away. You are the
      substance of my mind,
are my mind. And my spirit.
And flesh.

Ah! There you are — right
  in me through and through
and through. More of course.
Infinitely more. But we are of
    the same nature. You did say
      that, too, didn't you?

When then, because of your
love, in response to your
love, any of us,
belonging to you, express
your love, that action
is right for everyone. Some-
thing more of you is loosed
into the world. *You* become
more. And others whom we
do not know so touched
become more. As we.

So you
   who are
      grace and
         mystery and
            power and
               truth and
                  love
I adore
   adore
      adore
         you.

Identity

You, Christ, are
  now in me
To deal with me
  as you want to.

I give myself (again)
  to you who are
    the core of my being.

You only will I serve
  (I pray)
You only can make me.

I am here to glorify
  you
So let my eye be set on
  you
      Lord Christ.

Presence

Your presence, Lord,
  within me —
More powerful
  more present
More personal
  judging, loving
    real
      than ever.

My companion
  now
I thank you
  welcome you.

Come, Lord Jesus
  come, rest, be
  within me.

There grow
  until between
me and thee
  there is no
separation but one
  will only.

Fire

Good morning
  God.
You came to me
  last night
A vivid presence
  burning.

Today you are
  calmer, more
  pervasive, quiet
   here.

So I go with you
  today
responding, I pray,
  to you alone

So that you — flaming
  or quietly — may
through me
  be seen by those
   who see me.

The Swing

It's sitting on a
    trapeze, Lord, pumping
away, letting it swing,
    buffeted, blown, the old
cat dies, and over again
up and up and up.

Hanging on, knowing it
    will never break.

The bar alone to
    hang on. The ropes
above, out of sight, beyond
the canvas, anchored there
    out of sight, firm, secure . . .

so you believe, and so
    you trust.

All you can do is trust
    what is above is beyond
    sight, beyond control — and
nobody's business but God's
    if there be God.
So I sit and swing, pull
    on the ropes, to go higher
        and higher

and sing to you
for you
and if you're
not there,
I'll put you there.

A Reminder

You promised me
   a stone
     Lord
and you kept
   your promise.

But you never
   mentioned
the waves that
   flood over
   me
tossing, tumbling
   me
until they break
   and pass.

Is that your love
   Lord
Reminding me
   You are God
   I a creature
   not God?

Currents

Lord God
  great, holy
become
  small, lonely
tumbling over
  your creation
stirring currents of air
  by your presence

so in your absence
  we may breathe
  more freely.

Frail Stuff

Pretty frail stuff,
　Lord,
You have to work with
　in me.

Yet you knew this
　when you put me
　　here — even before
I was.

So why waste time
　complaining
about my nature
　when it was
Your nature to call
　me to take on
　　yours
As you did mine
　so that I might
by loving myself
　love you?

Slash

Slash,
   the knife
   cuts
the air
   the face,
    the heart
pouring of blood
   stains,
    dries
life gone
   for what purpose
this death?

"God knows"
   we say
    God
and you aren't
   saying
anything
   except you're
   God.

Silence

How come,
 Lord
You speak
 in silence
best?

No word
 made flesh
 except
in mine?

No love
 expressed
  except
in mine?

No sacrifice
 or strength
 given
except in what I give?

So in my silence
 I hear you
  speak
silently, silently.

I keep silence.

Holding On

Hold on
   to you
      you are.

Quiet within
centered into
   the depths
of who you
   are.

Let then
   arise
what
   has to
be

Then no question
   who you are.

On Retreat

You brought me
  here, Lord
to meet you
  again

So I wait now
  for your
    move.

May my waiting
  be patient
  and expectant

My confidence
  has to be
    in you
for where else
  is my hope
but in you
  only?

So, come in
  your time,
    Lord Jesus.

Junk

Whence comes
 this anger,
this restlessness
 from deep
  within me?

This goddamn
self-righteousness,
 pretentiousness?

Some deep well
 deep within me
  spewing out all this
  junk.

I offer you
 all this,
— myself.

You can live it —
 you were made sin —
So I don't have to
 anymore.

It's yours.
 So am I.

Longing

So, these waves
  of longing that
flood me
  are you?
Not just from you
  but *you?*

My longing is
  your love
Turned inside
  out.
Don't let me fight longing
  then but
    embrace it.

And don't let me look
  to any person to
    meet that longing
To put on a person
  only what you
    can do.

You may give people
who love
but they aren't
God
any more than
I am
God knows
(and so they)

Since you put
that longing
there
only you can meet
it with your love.

Thank you for loved ones
for whom I long
In your love I am
free to love them
best.

Honor

What I really
  want
is to praise, honor
  and glorify
  you.
Why in God's name
  don't I do it?

That other law in
  my members,
Screw it.

If I continue to
  have this intention
to honor you (as
  you honor me)
then you will
  enable me to
    do it.
I trust.

Friend Or Enemy

Come on,
  God,
are you friend
  or enemy?

You comfort
  me
and desert
  me.

You exalt
  me
and terrify
  me.

You give me
  joy
and I have a
  deep sense
of dread
  when I think
  of you
and when I don't.

You fill me
  up
and leave me
  empty.

Your absence is
   more your state
than your presence.

I hate dealing
   with you
and I love
   you.

I wish you would
   die
and I yearn for
life eternal.

Are you friend
   or enemy?
Which am I?

Terror

"He meant to pass by them."
—MARK 6:48b

Why did you want to
do that, Lord?
Why pass them by
when you saw that
they were distressed in
rowing, for the wind
was against them?
What kind of leadership
is that? What was
in your mind?

The need to be alone. You put
them in the boat, shoved it
off the beach, dismissed the
crowd, went into the hills to
pray.

Your need you gave up because
they "were terrified."

In my terror when I cry to you
may I also hear your words, "Take
heart, it is I: have no fear."

Yet down deep, Lord,
    way down deep, I am afraid —
    Awed by you.
So the terror
    you placed there
That I may find you.

Darkness

"Darkness is my only companion."
—PSALM 88:19b

Can't grope
   in the darkness
Lord. Nothing to hold
   on to.
Can bump
   barked shins
Touch the edges
   sometimes
but most time
   no limits
Just infinite space
   infinite darkness.

And darkness
   inside
That interior
   abyss
black, bleak
   nothing
no bottom
   no end
     me.

Darkness and light
   are both alike
     to you, Lord.

Let me then
  patiently wait
upon you to
  lead me to the
    light.

In the darkness
  is my companion
and you.

Good Friday

May I be so
oned
with you
today
that I let
go
all my self,
will, passions
ego
to be broken
by and for
love of
you
and so be freed
from myself
to live freely
in you,
you.

Holy Saturday

Entombed
  you wait
for the Spirit
  to blow
that rock
  away.

So may I wait in
  my darkness
    attentive
  to the wind
    stirring
new life
      within.

Easter Monday

Christ raised
from the dead
to move over
dead bodies
dead emotions
dead lands
dead people
so they might
mourn.

So for Christ's sake
don't ever
give up.

Keep moving
so you might
bring new life
to the dying
dead
ones.

Soaring

To be free
  in you
    O Lord
is to rise from
  the depths
and soar
  through
    life,
loving whom
  you give
  one
    with
      them
whole.

You are the
  one
I am oned
  with
whole, free
  soaring.

A Little While

"A little while," you said
  "and you will see me
    no more; again a little while,
    and you will see me."

So now you have come
  and will come again.
    In between I
      wait. We wait. We all
      wait.

You wait also
  for you are
    with us
We wait together.
For what? For whom?
    you.

So come, Lord Jesus,
  come.

In you, with you
  you have come
    into me
So since you have overcome
    the world
in it I rejoice. And sing.

"All Shall Be Well"

*"Sin is [inevitable] but all shall
be well, and all shall be well, and all
manner of thing shall be well."*
—DAME JULIAN OF NORWICH

My longing for you
    Lord
is your love
    for me

Prayer is my
    longing
and your
    love.

To give up
    prayer
is to give up.

Continuing prayer
    is to continue
        hoping

So may my
    longings never
        cease
and all shall be well.

Birth

Pain and birth
  birth and joy
Why, Lord,
  that sequence?

New life
  creation,
   hope,
expectation
  all rise out
of the messy
  mix of
  blood,
    love,
      cutting,
    waiting
      trusting
        holding onto
one another
  and you
Just like you
  giving a new creation
    new birth
with the pain of the cross.

Union

Lord Jesus
   above the heavens
    amongst us
     within me

Source of life
  who renews life
goads us, pulls, waits:
  grace

Mysterious, baffling,
  beyond touching
    more real than hands
pull me into you
  penetrate me
  I, you
  One

Aching

So long
    too long

my heart aches.
Longing
    is love
human
for divine.

You long,
    love
for human
    response

In your time
    with your grace
we meet in love
    and now
        wait
    in hope.

Job

Oh that I
   knew where
I might find
   him.

He has come,
   is here
has found you

So be.
   Accept the self/selves
   that you are
   others. God

He has found,
   accepted you
   — them.

So you.

Flux

Look at blackness
   till it changes,
lightens, turns
   to white.

Look at whiteness
   till it changes,
blues, whirls yellow
   green and back
      again.

So in the flux
   of everything
the changes
   themselves
are you
   constant, eternal.

Tantalizer

You tantalize
  Jesus

You come suddenly
  and so leave

You beckon
  and hide at
    the same time

You flash into view
  and skip away

You are here
  all the time
so that when I
  don't see you
I may praise you

Almighty, eternal
  invisible
    One

Eternity

There, through
   the opening cut
   of the trees,
     the sea, sparkling
on this clear as crystal
morning
   and beyond the horizon,
deep blue sea, a wave
flickers, light blue sky meet,
   a white cloud hovering
   branches of pine, grass
of dunes bend gently,
return under soft breeze
   and you, O Lord, are
where?
   Everywhere,
   I pray,
   and here in
   my heart.

JOHN B. COBURN is the Episcopal Bishop of Massachusetts. He was formely Dean of the Episcopal Theological School and the Rector of St. James Church in New York City. Bishop Coburn is the author of many books, including *The Hope of Glory, Deliver Us from Evil, Christ's Life: Our Life, A Life to Live — A Way to Pray, Prayer and Personal Religion,* and *Anne and the Sand Dobbies.* The present volume is his first public collection of poetry.

A note about the type used in this book: The text is set in 12 on 13 point *Garamond* through the linotype method of typesetting by Southern New England Typographic Service in Hamden, Connecticut. *Garamond* is a classic Old Style face — with graduated thick and thin strokes and slanted serifs — based upon the design of the French type founder Claude Garamond in 1540.